From Egg to Adult
The Life Cycle of Amphibians

Heinemann
LIBRARY

Richard and Louise Spilsbury

www.heinemann.co.uk/library
Visit our website to find out more information about **Heinemann Library** books.

To order:
☎ Phone 44 (0) 1865 888066
🖹 Send a fax to 44 (0) 1865 314091
🖥 Visit the Heinemann Bookshop at www.heinemann.co.uk/library to browse our
catalogue and order online.

First published in Great Britain by Heinemann
Library, Halley Court, Jordan Hill, Oxford OX2 8EJ,
a division of Harcourt Education Ltd.
Heinemann is a registered trademark of Harcourt
Education Ltd.

Editorial: Nicole Irving and Georga Godwin
Design: Jo Hinton-Malivoire and AMR
Illustrations: David Woodroffe
Picture Research: Maria Joannou and Lizz Eddison
Production: Séverine Ribierre

Originated by Dot Gradations Ltd
Printed in China by Wing King Tong

ISBN 0 431 16865 2
07 06 05 04 03
10 9 8 7 6 5 4 3 2 1

**British Library Cataloguing in Publication
Data**
Spilsbury, Richard and Spilsbury, Louise
From egg to adult: The life cycle of amphibians
571.81178
A full catalogue record for this book is available
from the British Library.

Acknowledgements
The Publishers would like to thank the following
for permission to reproduce photographs:
Ardea/Peter Steyn p. **16**; Bruce Coleman
Collection/Jane Burton pp. **5, 6, 15**; Bruce
Coleman/Kim Taylor p. **8**; FLPA/Minden Pictures
p. **26**; FLPA/Treat Davidson p. **12a**; NHPA/Ant
Photo Library p. **22**; NHPA/Daniel Heuclin pp. **19,
24**; NHPA/James Carmichael Jr p. **10**; NHPA/Karl
Switak p. **13**; NHPA/Roger Tidman p. **20**;
NHPA/Stephen Dalton pp. **11, 14, 25**; Oxford
Scientific Films pp. **9b, 21**; Oxford Scientific
Films/Juan M Renjifo p. **17**; Oxford Scientific
Films/Mantis Wildlife Films p. **18**; Oxford Scientific
Films/Marty Cordano p. **12b**; Oxford Scientific
Films/P J Devries p. **23**; Oxford Sceintific
Films/Paulo De Oliveira p. **7**.

Cover photograph of the common frogs
reproduced with permission of Bruce Coleman
Collection.

The frog at the top of each page is a red-eyed
tree frog.

The authors would like to thank their teachers for
all their help and support.

The Publishers would like to thank Colin Fountain
for his assistance in the preparation of this book.

Every effort has been made to contact copyright
holders of any material reproduced in this book.
Any omissions will be rectified in subsequent
printings if notice is given to the Publishers.

Disclaimer
All the Internet addresses (URLs) given in this book
were valid at the time of going to press. However,
due to the dynamic nature of the Internet, some
addresses may have changed, or sites may have
changed or ceased to exist since publication. While
the author and Publishers regret any inconvenience
this may cause readers, no responsibility for any such
changes can be accepted by either the author or
the Publishers.

Contents

Look but don't touch: many amphibians are delicate but also have poisonous skin. If you see one in the wild, do not go too close to it. Look at it, but do not touch it!

Any words appearing in bold, **like this**, are explained in the Glossary.

What is an amphibian?

Amphibians are animals, such as frogs, that usually live both in water and on land during their lives. Amphibians have soft skin without scales or hair. The skin is usually covered in **mucus** to keep it moist. Most amphibians breathe partly through their moist skin and partly through lungs or **gills**.

Amphibians are **vertebrates** – this means that just like us, they have a backbone supporting their body. Unlike us, they are cold-blooded, which means their bodies are only as warm or cold as the places they live in.

common frog

tiger salamander

caecilian

Three groups of amphibians

There are over 4000 different **species** of amphibians on Earth. They are divided into three groups – frogs and toads, salamanders and newts and caecilians.

This shows the three groups of amphibians when they are fully grown. Frogs and toads have no tails, large heads and eyes and long back legs. Newts and salamanders look a bit like lizards, with tails, small eyes and usually equal length limbs. Caecilians (or 'blind worms') have no eyes, no legs and usually no tail. They look much more like giant earthworms or snakes than frogs!

How are amphibians born?

When baby amphibians are born they usually **hatch** – come out – from eggs. These eggs are round and less than 1 centimetre across. The middle of the egg is the **yolk**. Part of the yolk develops into an **embryo**, which becomes the baby amphibian. The embryo becomes bigger and stronger by using the rest of the yolk as food.

Protective covering

The outer covering of an amphibian egg is usually soft, clear and like jelly. This covering helps protect the developing embryo against being knocked. It also helps it from drying out – if embryos dry out they usually die.

These are frog eggs. The black spot in the middle is the yolk that will develop into a young frog.

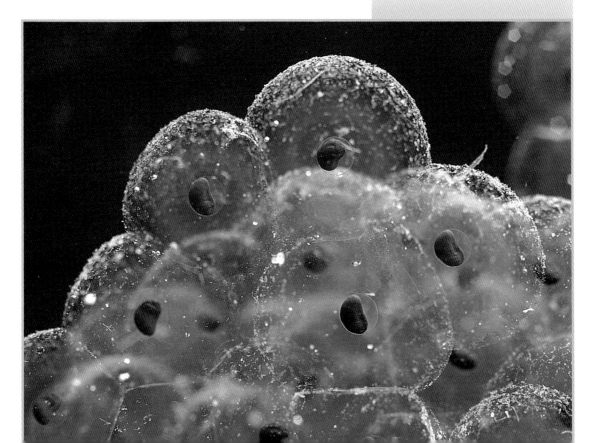

Amphibians lay their eggs in wet places, such as the calm waters of a pond. This helps to stop them getting dry. The eggs are sticky so that they stick to each other, water plants or rocks and stay safe.

Some amphibians, such as toads, lay their eggs in sticky strings about a metre long. Some, such as frogs, produce hundreds or even thousands of eggs that cling together in floating masses of jelly called frogspawn. Others lay much smaller numbers of eggs.

Some amphibians, such as the common toad, wrap their strings of eggs around water plants so the eggs do not drift away.

Breaking free

It takes around two weeks for most amphibian embryos to develop fully. Some amphibians may take longer to develop than others. The weather can affect the time development takes. If it is too cold, eggs may take much longer to hatch. In hot, dry places where ponds only appear for a short time after a rainy season, it may take months before it is wet enough for eggs to hatch.

When they are ready to hatch, the **larvae** wriggle and twist. This movement breaks open the jelly covering around the eggs and the larvae emerge.

Salamander larvae wriggle to break out of their eggs.

Odd ones out

Some frogs, salamanders and caecilians give birth to live young. The eggs stay inside the female's body and the embryos develop there, protected from the world outside. The young are actually born after they have hatched from their eggs inside her.

What do new baby amphibians look like?

Many amphibian larvae look like tiny fish when they hatch. Frog and toad larvae are usually called tadpoles or polliwogs. A tadpole that has just hatched is just a few millimetres long. Its head and body form a wide lump with a narrow tail attached. It has no legs or arms. Two or three pairs of feathery **gills** grow behind its head.

Breathing underwater with gills

Most amphibian larvae and all fish have gills to breathe underwater. Gills contain **blood vessels** surrounded by thin skin. Water contains dissolved **oxygen**, a gas that nearly all animals need to breathe to live. When water flows over gills, oxygen goes into the blood vessels. Blood carries the oxygen to parts of an animal's body that need it. It also helps to take away wastes from the animal's body.

A newt larva is a similar shape to an adult, but it has three pairs of gills and no proper legs. As the larva grows up, it changes.

Who looks after baby amphibians?

Most amphibians never know their parents. After the eggs are laid and **fertilized**, the parents go elsewhere, often out of the water. The **larvae** are left on their own.

Dangers

Life is very dangerous for amphibian larvae. Most of them do not survive their first few days or weeks. They are small and weak, so they cannot move quickly, nor can they see much. This makes it easy for **predators**, such as fish, to catch and eat them.

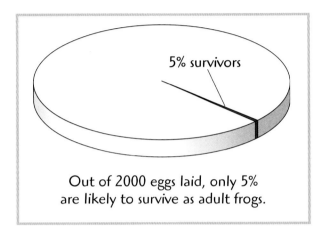

5% survivors

Out of 2000 eggs laid, only 5% are likely to survive as adult frogs.

Staying alive

Larvae usually stay still at first to try to avoid being spotted. Common frog larvae attach themselves to water plants, often in the shade. They feed at first on the **yolk** left over in their stomachs (bellies) from their time inside the eggs.

Common frog larvae cling on to plants for safety, by using special suckers behind their mouths.

sucker

A safer start

A few amphibians look after their young larvae to give them a safer start to life out of the egg. This takes time and energy, but means the youngsters are more likely to grow up to become adults.

Some frogs carry their larvae until they are big enough to survive on their own. Mouth or stomach 'brooders' carry their young inside their mouths or stomachs. After Darwin's frog tadpoles have hatched, the father swallows them! He is not eating them – just providing a safe, moist place where his young can spend their first few days.

The tadpole of this arrow-poison frog clings to its parent's back using its sucker.

Model mum

The female spot-bellied dart frog lays three or four eggs on the moist ground in the **rainforest**. When they hatch, she carries the tadpoles on her back to tiny pools of water in the centre of **bromeliad** plants growing up trees. She then lays eggs in the water for the tadpoles to eat.

How do baby amphibians grow bigger?

Amphibian **larvae** need to find food to grow bigger. As they grow, the larvae also gradually change shape. This is called **metamorphosis**.

Body changes

In frogs and toads, the adults look totally different from the tadpoles. The tadpole has a long tail **adapted** for swimming in water, and no legs. The adult frog or toad has no tail but has legs to walk, hop or crawl – so that it can live on land.

In many salamanders and caecilians, larvae and adults look very similar to each other, except for their size. This is because when they **hatch** they are already adapted to the place where they will spend all their lives.

*Some salamanders, such as this axolotl, and some mudpuppies live in water all their lives – from egg to adult. They have **gills** throughout their lives and some grow only tiny legs.*

During metamorphosis, a bullfrog tadpole's tail gradually starts to disappear and its back legs start to appear. A flap of skin grows over its gills, and lungs develop inside. The bullfrog can then breathe out of water.

By the time it is ready to leave the water, the young frog's front legs have grown. Its head, eyes and mouth are bigger, and its back legs have lengthened and strengthened. It has **webbed** feet to help it swim when it visits ponds or pools.

From plants to meat

Most amphibian larvae start off as **herbivores**, but during metamorphosis they become **carnivores**. At first, frog and toad tadpoles graze on water plants using their rough lips to 'sandpaper' bits off. They become strong enough to swim faster and gradually start to catch floating and swimming food such as water fleas. Their jaws change shape so they can catch food, and their stomachs change to be able to digest meat. Salamander and newt larvae are carnivores from the moment they hatch.

What do amphibians eat?

Adult amphibians generally catch insects, spiders, small fish, worms and slugs. Larger amphibian species such as bullfrogs may eat snakes, small mammals and birds. Some amphibians only eat particular food. One group of South American frogs feeds mainly on other types of frogs, but another eats mostly fruit.

This Argentine horned frog is eating a young Argentine rainbow boa.

Catching food

Most amphibians, such as giant salamanders, sit and wait for **prey** to come closer, but some toads and salamanders **stalk** their food. Many caecilians burrow through soil and find food as they go. Frogs and toads usually flick out their sticky tongues to catch prey, but some use their hands. Amphibians have no chewing teeth so they always swallow food whole.

When amphibians, such as this Bell's horned frog, push down their eyeballs, they help to squeeze larger meals down their throat.

Using their senses

Amphibians use different **senses** to help them find food, depending on where they live. Frogs and toads have good hearing, and most adult amphibians have good eyesight to spot a potential meal. Eyes are useless to **burrowing** caecilians and cave salamanders that live in the dark – they rely on touch to find food. Many amphibians can breathe in smells in the air, which they taste using special **pits** (called Jacobson's organ) in their mouths.

How do amphibians grow up safely?

Amphibians face many dangers as they grow up. One of the biggest dangers is a **predator**. Many birds, fish and reptiles rely on amphibians as food.

A quick getaway

If they sense danger, many amphibians can get away quickly. Most adult frogs have long, strong legs so they can jump away – up to 3 metres at a time! Flying frogs use their **webbed** toes like parachutes to glide from tree to tree.

Fighting back

Some amphibians try to frighten off predators. Large amphibians such as bullfrogs and hellbender salamanders often attack predators. The skunk frog of Venezuela makes horrible smelling **mucus** to put off attackers. Some newts and salamanders twist their bodies and lie still, pretending to be dead.

Common toads stand on tiptoes and suck in air to make themselves look bigger and fiercer.

Clever colours

Most amphibians use skin colour to avoid predators. Some are **camouflaged** – they are similar colours to the places where they live. Bright green tree frogs live among green leaves in trees. The Solomon Island leaf frog is similar in colour and shape to the brown, dead leaves it lives among.

Other amphibians are brightly coloured to warn predators not to eat them. For example, young eastern newts are bright red, and fire salamanders are black and yellow. These colours are very easy to see and **advertise** that they have a skin that produces poisonous or bad-tasting slime. Predators eating such a meal for the first time usually spit it out because it tastes so bad. They remember the horrible taste, and in the future are likely to avoid this coloured food.

The arum frog is white to hide in the new white flowers of arum lilies, but it turns brown as the flower fades and changes colour.

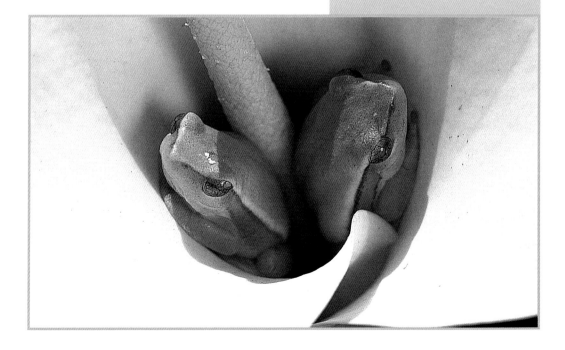

Keeping moist

Another big danger to amphibians is their skin drying out, especially if they live in hot places on land. Amphibians do not drink through their mouths – water mainly enters their bodies through their skin. To keep moist, most amphibians are active at night, when it is cooler, and hide in damp, cool places by day.

Keeping cool

Some amphibians find shelter from the heat in **burrows** dug by other animals, in drainpipes or under logs. Others dig their own shelters. Spadefoot toads use their shovel-shaped feet and dig down feet-first, but shovel-nosed frogs dig head-first.

Caecilians have tough skulls and pointed heads shaped for burrowing through the soil.

Ways of breathing

Amphibians breathe partly through lungs or **gills**, but also through their skin. If their thin skin is moist, **oxygen** from the air can pass through it and move into the blood. The blood carries the oxygen to the parts of the body that need it.

Taking a break

Some amphibians take a break from hot or cold seasons by going underground. When the air is cold, soil stays warmer, and when air is hot, soil stays cooler. The Australian water-holding frog lives in deserts where it may only rain once every seven years. It lives in a burrow for most of its life, only coming out when rainwater soaks the soil around it.

Surviving winter

Amphibians are cold-blooded. If there is no warmth from the sun, they have no energy to move around. Some, such as wood frogs, survive cold winters by **hibernating**. As they lie still in burrows under the frozen Arctic soil, their bodies shut down – they breathe slowly and do not eat – until spring. A special type of sugar in their blood stops their bodies freezing.

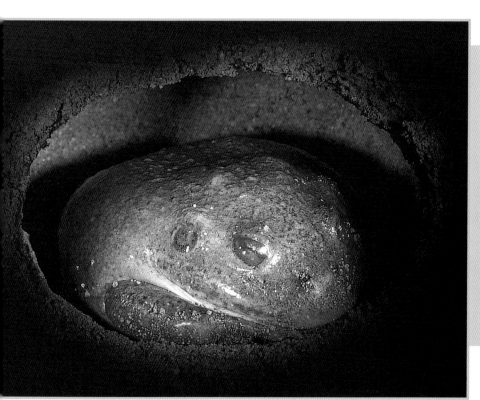

*The Australian water–holding frog survives underground using water stored in its body, safe in a protective **cocoon** made of its own **shed** skin.*

When are amphibians grown up?

An amphibian is 'grown up' when it can start **breeding** – when its body is ready to have young of its own. In some amphibians this can take just a few weeks, or months, after **metamorphosis**, but most take longer. Common frogs take three years, but newts take about two years.

Growing up quickly

Different amphibian **species** develop at different rates, but the speed also depends on where they live. For example, in places where pools of water collect only for a short time, amphibian young have to grow up quickly.

Slowing up

Amphibians grow much more quickly during metamorphosis than after they are grown up. Adults do not need to eat as much or as often as when they are young and developing rapidly.

Chinese giant salamanders take about ten years to grow up. After that, they continue to grow slowly as they get older.

How do amphibians have babies?

When it is grown up, a male amphibian finds a female to **mate** with. Most amphibians' eggs and swimming **larvae** need to live in water, so most grown-up amphibians mate in wet places. They mate at times of year when it is particularly wet, but also warm enough for their young to develop quickly.

Breeding places

Amphibians that live mostly on land find water by sensing how damp the air is, by smell, but also by having a good sense of direction. Some amphibian adults return to the same wet places year after year, sometimes after long **migrations**. Sometimes these are the same places they were born. Great crested newts migrate up to 10 km (6 miles) to get to **breeding** ponds.

The migration routes of common toads sometimes go across roads, so in some places people put up special signs warning motorists to slow down.

Finding a mate

Frogs and toads listen out for similar calls to their own. If they follow these calls, they are more likely to find the right mate.

In some places, male amphibians set up a breeding **territory** – usually a sheltered area, to attract a female to lay her eggs. Males then defend this area by fighting or chasing other males away.

Showing off

Many male salamanders and newts put on **courtship** displays (special shows) to attract a mate. Some develop special breeding colours to make them more noticeable.

Perfumed partners

Axolotls are blind and deaf and live in dark underground pools. So, females produce a special smell that spreads through the water to attract males.

Great crested male newts have special bright silvery breeding colours on their tails and tall crests on their backs. The male lashes his tail back and forth to make sure a female sees him.

Calling for a partner

Frogs and toads have special courtship calls. Different **species** and individuals have different calls. Usually the male calls to attract a female. He inflates **vocal sacs** in his throat in order to make as loud a sound as possible. In a few species, it is the female that calls the male.

Calling could also attract **predators**. So most frogs and toads call at night under the cover of darkness.

Crafty males

Male frogs that make bigger sounds will attract more females. Sometimes smaller males hide near males with loud calls. They then catch any females attracted to the calls and mate with them.

The male coqui (you say ko-kee) tree frog of Puerto Rico gets its name from its loud two-part call. The 'kee' sound attracts females, but the 'ko' sound means 'keep away' to other males.

A big hug

Once they have found a female, most male amphibians make sure they do not lose her before she is ready to mate. They do this by hugging her tightly. Spanish sharp-ribbed salamander males hug their female for up to 24 hours.

Many male frogs and toads have patches of rough skin on their thumbs to get a better grip on slippery females.

At mating time, a female already has eggs inside her body ready to be laid. She lays the eggs in the water and the male **fertilizes** them by dropping his sperm on top.

Hitching a lift

Some male amphibians are much smaller than females of the same species. A red-eyed tree frog male calls from a tree to attract a female. When she approaches he grips onto her and hitches a lift to a nearby pond where they will mate.

The male red-eyed tree frog stays close to the female until she is ready to lay her eggs.

Protecting eggs

Some amphibians hide their eggs to protect them from predators. Grey tree frogs make sticky foam nests to hide their eggs in. Female newts lay about 80 sticky eggs and wrap each one up in a water plant leaf.

After a female marsupial frog lays her eggs, the male scoops them up into a pouch on her back where they stay until the tadpoles come out.

Many caecilians and salamanders coil their bodies around their eggs to guard them until they **hatch**.

Keeping eggs moist

Amphibians that lay eggs on land have to stop them drying up. Female barking frogs lay their eggs in cliff crevices and the males **urinate** (wee) on the eggs to keep them moist.

The female surinam toad lays about 50 eggs in water. The eggs stick to her back and her skin grows over them for protection.

How old do amphibians get?

Most amphibians never reach old age. At all stages in its life – from egg to **larva** to adult – an individual faces danger. As it gets older, it may pick up injuries from fights or close calls with **predators**. This often means it cannot move quickly enough to avoid predators and other dangers.

A long life

Some amphibians do live for a long time, mostly in captivity – such as in a zoo – where there are no predators. Some Japanese giant salamanders have lived up to 55 years in captivity, growing up to 180 cm long. Others may live even longer in wild places such as remote mountain rivers, which are also safe from danger.

Amphibians need to be aware of danger at all times.

Keeping up appearances

Amphibians, like all living things, **inherit** some things from their parents – for example, a frog usually looks like its parents. However, how it looks also depends on the **environment** it grows up in. If it grows up somewhere that is dry or without much food, it may be less healthy and smaller than its parents.

People and amphibians

There are some dangers that amphibians cannot avoid, whether they are young or old. People are destroying many of the wet places that amphibians live in. Marshes and bogs are being drained so that the land can be used for farming. Water from rivers and streams is taken to **irrigate** land and to use in factories. Many **rainforests** have been cut down for **timber**, or cleared to make land for farming.

Pollution in water and in the air from factories, farms and cars can kill many amphibians. Their moist skin easily soaks up pollution.

Disappearing acts

As different **habitats** are affected, many amphibians are becoming rare and may even become extinct. New types of amphibians are found each year, but it is likely that many more are disappearing without ever being discovered.

Water pollution is causing many frogs around the world to develop strangely shaped legs and eyes.

Life cycles

As amphibians slow down towards the end of their lives, they **breed** much less often and are less able to catch food. Finally, they die. The number of young an individual amphibian produces is more important to the **survival** of its **species** than how many years it lives.

Over a lifetime – if she has found suitable breeding places and males to **mate** with – a common toad female may have laid tens of thousands of eggs. Not all of these eggs will **hatch**, and not all the larvae will **metamorphose** into adults. Those that then survive the challenges that life brings – such as predators and drying out – may eventually breed themselves. This is the cycle of life – from egg to adult – in which young are born, grow and produce young themselves. This cycle of life ensures the survival of each amphibian species.

The life cycle of a poison-dart frog.

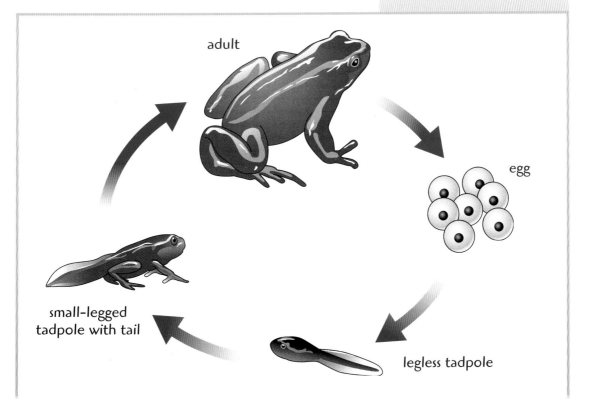

adult

egg

small-legged tadpole with tail

legless tadpole

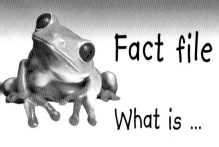

Fact file

What is ...

· the fastest metamorphosis?

Grey tree frogs take just one month to transform from egg to young frog, but mountain yellow-legged frogs may take three to four years if they live in cold water.

· the oldest individual?

The oldest toad (a common toad) was 40 years, and the oldest salamander (a Japanese giant salamander) was 55 years old.

· the biggest individual?

Species	Body length	Weight
Chinese giant salamander	180 cm	65 kg
Caecilian	150 cm	unknown
Goliath frog	30 cm	3.3 kg

· the smallest individual?

The smallest adult amphibian is a Brazilian frog (gold frog), which is less than 1 centimetre long.

What was the first amphibian?

From fossils, scientists have worked out that the first amphibians lived on Earth around 360 million years ago – earlier than dinosaurs. Amphibians were the first **vertebrates** to live on land.

Amphibian classification

Different amphibians can look as different as a tree frog and an axolotl. They are classified (grouped) together because they are similar in some ways, such as their naked (no scales or hairs) skin, their skeletons and the way they **breed** and change as they grow up. There are three amphibian families:

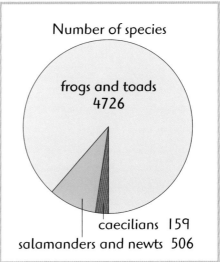

Number of species

frogs and toads
4726

caecilians 159

salamanders and newts 506

- Frogs and toads that all have large heads and short bodies.
  Toads are very much like frogs but their skin is rougher and their back legs are shorter.
- Salamanders and newts. Newts are just one type of salamander. Other types of salamander range from tiny ones with gripping tails that live up trees to giant salamanders that grow up to 1.5 metres long.
- Caecilians. Although these look more like big earthworms than frogs, caecilians are burrowing animals that have a lot of similarities with other amphibians.

Within each family there are smaller groups containing members that are similar in some way. For example, there are over 800 known **species** of tree frogs that are grouped together because they all have sticky fingers shaped for climbing trees.

Glossary

adapted when a plant or animal gradually changes over thousands of years to thrive in the habitat in which it lives

advertise draw attention to

blood vessels tube through which blood flows

breed have babies

bromeliad plant that grows on another plant for support, which collects rainwater in waxy leaves that form cups

burrowing digging underground

burrows animal homes that are dug underground

camouflage colour or pattern that helps an animal blend in with its background

carnivores meat-eating animals

cocoon protective covering

courtship special behaviour before mating

embryo unborn young

environment surroundings, including the place, plants and animals that live there

fertilize when an egg is fertilized, an embryo begins to grow inside

gills body parts used for breathing underwater

habitat place where a plant or animal lives. There are many different habitats in the world, such as a rainforest habitat.

hatch break out of an egg

herbivores animals that eat plants

hibernate deep sleep to avoid cold temperatures

inherit when an animal is born with features that are the same as their parents

irrigate when people make land wetter to grow crops by redirecting rivers and streams

larva young animal that looks very different to its parents, for example, a tadpole

mate what a male and female animal do to start a baby growing. An animal's mate is an animal of the other sex that they can have young with.

metamorphosis change of shape during an animal's life cycle

migration regular movement of animals from one place to another, usually in search for food or a place to breed

mucus slimy liquid produced by amphibians and other animals

oxygen gas in the air and dissolved in water, which living things need to breathe

predator animal that hunts or catches other animals to eat them

prey animals that are hunted or caught for food by predators

rainforest thick forests of tall trees that grow in hot places where it rains daily

senses ways in which animals see, hear, touch, smell and taste things

shed when animals lose and replace their skin

species type of living thing. Male and female animals of the same species can breed to produce healthy offspring.

stalk quietly and secretly hunt

survival staying alive

territory area within a habitat that an animal claims as its own

timber wood from trees used to make or build things with

urinate wee

vertebrates animals with backbones

vocal sac skin near throat that can expand to help an amphibian make sounds

webbed skin between the toes to help animals move through water

yolk part of an egg that is food for the embryo

Find out more

Books

Frog, Michael Chinery (Eagle Books, 1991)

Eyewitness Guide: Amphibian, Barry Clarke (Dorling Kindersley, 1993)

What is an amphibian?, Robert Sneddon (Belitha Press, 1993)

Frogs, Toads and Treefrogs: Everything about Selection, Care, Nutrition, Breeding, and Behavior, Patricia Bartlett and R. D. Bartlett (Barvous Educational, 1996)

Websites

Froggy facts and fun:
http://www.allaboutfrogs.org/froglnd.shtml
http://www.allaboutfrogs.org/weird/weird.html

AmphibiaWeb – more detailed information about amphibians of the world:
http://www.elib.cs.berkeley.edu/aw/

Amphibians from the point of view of visitors from other planets:
http://www.alienexplore.com/ecology/topic15.html

Index